Hanukkah Around the World

by Tami Lehman-Wilzig

illustrations by Vicki Wehrman

KAR-BEN
PUBLISHING

Dedicated to my husband Sam, a true guiding light.

I also want to thank all those who shared their customs with me and put up with my constant nudging about details: Rabbi Raymond Apple, Rabbi Mendel Kastel, Klara Lindell, Mina Shomron, Rabbi Alberto Somech, Alex and Nili Weinreb, Sarah Yokhananov and Olga Zambrofsky. — T.L.W.

Dedicated to all of life's teachers. — V.W.

Text copyright © 2009 by Tami Lehman-Wilzig
Illustrations copyright © 2009 by Lerner Publishing Group

Kar-Ben Publishing, Inc.
A division of Lerner Publishing Group, Inc.
241 First Avenue North
Minneapolis, Minnesota 55401 U.S.A.
800-4KARBEN

Website address: www.karben.com

Library of Congress Cataloging-in-Publication Data

Lehman-Wilzig, Tami.
    Hanukkah around the world/by Tami Lehman-Wilzig ; illustrations by Vicki Wehrman.
       p. cm.
    ISBN 978-0-8225-8761-3 (lib. bdg. : alk. paper)
    1. Hanukkah—Juvenile literature. I. Wehrman, Vicki. II. Title
BM695.H3L37 2009
296.4'3509—dc22   2008031196

Manufactured in the United States of America
1 2 3 4 5 6 7 — DP — 14 13 12 11 10 09

Contents

HANUKKAH
The Holiday That Lights Up Our Life

Hanukkah is a happy holiday filled with songs, games, and gifts. All over the world, Jews gather to light and bless the holiday candles and to recall the story of religious freedom that is behind all the fun.

The first Hanukkah was celebrated over 2,000 years ago. At that time, Israel was ruled by Syrian Greeks. Their king, Antiochus Epiphanes, wanted the Jews to accept Greek culture. When he used the Holy Temple for pagan sacrifices, the Jews knew they had to take a stand.

Enter the Maccabees. Their fight began in Modi'in, where a priest named Mattathias lived with his five sons. He decided that Antiochus had to be stopped and appointed his third son, Judah, to lead the rebellion. Judah was given the name Maccabee. Some say the name is from the Aramaic word for "hammer," and hammer away is exactly what Judah did. He understood strategy. He and his small band of fighters pounded the large Syrian army for three years. Eventually they drove the enemy out of Jerusalem and restored the Temple. On the 25th day of the Jewish month of Kislev in the year 165 B.C.E., the golden menorah in the Temple was relit. The people celebrated joyfully for eight days and proclaimed that they would celebrate a holiday of rededication each year.

Hanukkah is a celebration of miracles. The first miracle is that a small army, with few weapons, was able to win against the large, well-trained Syrian army.

The second miracle concerns the little jug of oil. According to legend, when the Maccabees searched for the pure oil needed to light the Temple menorah, they found only one jug, enough to burn for just one day. But the oil lasted, and the menorah burned brightly for eight days until more oil could be found.

The Hanukkah-Israel Connection

In 1948, over 2,000 years after the first Hanukkah, the newly created State of Israel was at war. Once again, a small number of Jews relied on strategy to beat not one, but many mighty armies surrounding them. Like the victory of the Maccabees, Israel's victory was also a miracle. To honor it, the new Jewish state chose as its symbol the seven-branched Temple menorah.

What Does the Word *Hanukkah* Mean?

Hanukkah means dedication, which is exactly what the Jews did — they rededicated the Temple and made it holy again. Today, when members of a family move, they often host a *Hanukkat HaBayit* to dedicate their new home. This housewarming includes putting mezuzahs on the doorposts and rejoicing with family and friends.

Hanukkah is also called Chag Ha'or — the holiday of light. We place the hanukkiah near a window to proclaim the miracle, and so that neighbors and passersby can see, admire, and share in its light.

The *Hanukkiah*

In Hebrew, the Hanukkah menorah is called a *hanukkiah*. Unlike the seven-branched Temple menorah, it has nine branches – eight to recall the miracle of the oil and an extra, the *shamash*, to light the others.

Candles or Oil?

Those who wish to remain true to the miracle of Hanukkah use pure olive oil with cotton wicks to light the hanukkiah. Other oils and wicks, or wax candles, may also be used. The lights must stay lit for at least half an hour, and no work should be done while they are burning. One needs 44 candles for all eight nights. Candles (or wicks) should be lined up from right to left. But the last candle added is the first lit, and the lighting continues from left to right. On Friday night, Hanukkah candles are lit before Shabbat candles. On Saturday night, Hanukkah candles are lit after Havdalah.

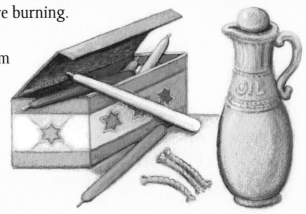

The Great Debate

Back in the 1st century, the famous rabbinic schools of Hillel and Shammai debated the order of lighting the Hanukkah menorah. According to Shammai's followers, we should kindle eight lights on the first night and one fewer each succeeding night, representing the gradual depletion of the little jug of pure oil. Hillel's students believed the opposite: we should begin with a single light and add one more each night, because the symbol of holiness should grow. The school of Hillel won the debate, and we continue to follow that order.

It's Time for Song

It is traditional to sing two songs after lighting the candles: *Hanerot Halalu* (These Lights) is based on a Talmudic text that explains that the lights are lit to recall the miracle. They are sacred and may not be used in any other way. An Ashkenazi custom is to follow with *Maoz Tzur* (Rock of Ages). Each of the song's stanzas praises God for rescuing the Jews from their many enemies throughout history. The fifth stanza recalls the miracle of Hanukkah.

The Hanukkah Megillah

There is no mention of Hanukkah in the Bible. The story is recorded in the *Books of the Maccabees* and referred to in the Talmud. Pieces of these texts and other legends about the holiday were compiled in The Scroll (*Megillah*) of Antiochus. Written in Aramaic sometime before the Middle Ages, it was translated into Hebrew and included in some prayer books. From the 9th century, it was read in a number of Jewish communities on the Shabbat that falls during Hanukkah.

Spin the Dreidel

Dreidel, a game of chance, is everyone's favorite Hanukkah pastime. There are different versions of the origins of the game. Legend dates it back to the actual time of the Hanukkah miracle, when Jews played dreidel as a way to hide their study of Torah. As soon as they saw Greek-Syrian soldiers approach, they put away their books, took out their dreidels, and pretended to play.

Some believe that the dreidel is a variation of a German gambling game, and that dreidel, which is a Yiddish word, comes from the German word *drehen* which means "to spin." In Hebrew, a dreidel is called a *sevivon*, which means "a spinning top."

The four letters on the dreidel **Nun, Gimel, Hey, Shin** stand for the words **Nes Gadol Hayah Sham** – A Great Miracle Happened There.

In Israel, the letter *Shin* is replaced by the letter **Peh**, reminding everyone that *Nes Gadol Hayah* **Poh** – A Great Miracle Happened Here.

Caesarea, an Israeli town along the Mediterranean coast, is home to the largest dreidel in the world. Created by Eran Greble, it is 18 feet tall and stands at the city's train station. Made out of a half ton of iron, it spins with the wind.

Let's Play

Players begin with an equal number of tokens, such as chocolate Hanukkah coins, pennies, or buttons. Each player puts a token into the middle. The first player spins the dreidel. If it lands on:

Nun – **N**o luck! No one collects.

Gimel – **G**ood for you! You get it all.

Hey – **H**alf is yours!

Shin – **S**hell out another token and add it to the pot.

Peh (on the Israeli dreidel) – **P**ut one in.

Before the next player spins, everyone must put in another token. The game ends when one person has accumulated all the tokens – or everyone is ready for latkes.

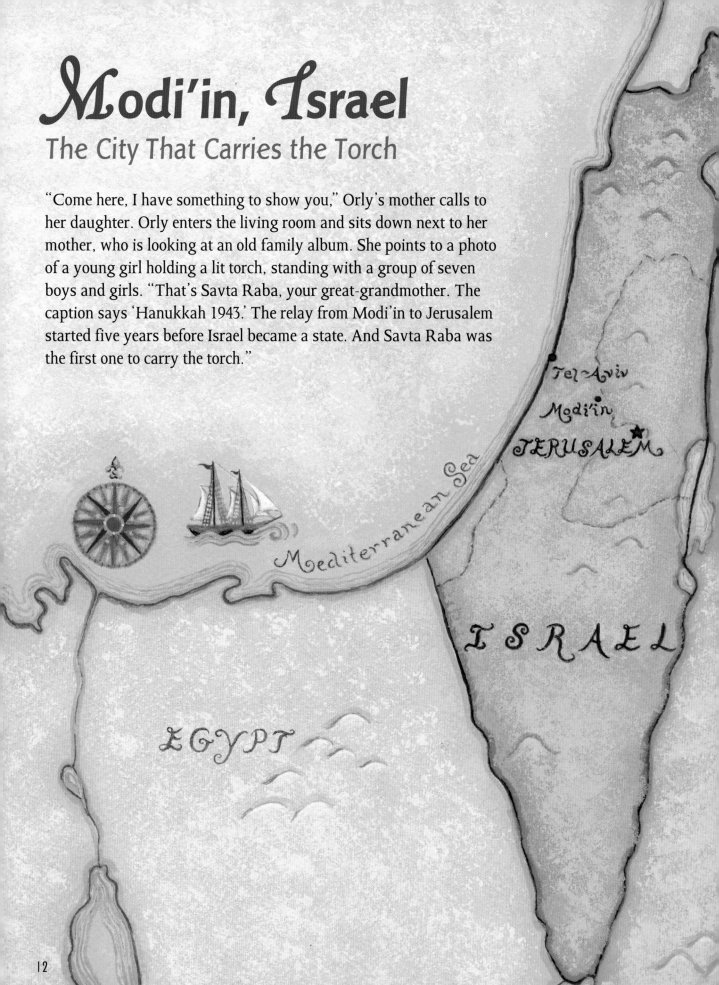

Modi'in, Israel
The City That Carries the Torch

"Come here, I have something to show you," Orly's mother calls to her daughter. Orly enters the living room and sits down next to her mother, who is looking at an old family album. She points to a photo of a young girl holding a lit torch, standing with a group of seven boys and girls. "That's Savta Raba, your great-grandmother. The caption says 'Hanukkah 1943.' The relay from Modi'in to Jerusalem started five years before Israel became a state. And Savta Raba was the first one to carry the torch."

Tel-Aviv

Modi'in

JERUSALEM

Mediterranean Sea

ISRAEL

EGYPT

Orly stares at the old black-and-white photo. "Wow! And this year I'm carrying the torch," she whispers.

Ima hugs Orly. "And you're carrying on a family tradition. When I visited Savta Raba and told her that you were chosen to lead the Hanukkah relay, she gave me this album, so you could see her photo."

The doorbell rings. "Come on in," Orly calls to her friend Anat. "Look at this!"Orly opens the album and tells Anat the story.

"Cool!" says Anat. She looks at her watch. "Oh, it's 3:15. We have to run. Today they're taking us to where the relay begins and showing us the route. We're starting near the graves of the Maccabees."

In a flash, the two are out the door. Seconds later Orly flies back in, panting. "Ima can I take the photo? I want to show it to Avi, my youth group leader."

Orly's mother carefully removes the photo and puts it in an envelope. "Just don't lose it!" she says.

Like Jerusalem, Modi'in is a perfect example of a Biblical city that's come alive. Located between Jerusalem and Tel Aviv, the ancient home of the Maccabees was reestablished as a city of the future in the 1990s. Architect Moshe Safdie designed the city's many parks, playgrounds, and beautiful homes to appeal to the family-friendly city of 70,000, a third of whom are children. In 2004, the city council passed a law making Hanukkah the city's official holiday. In 2007, Modi'in was one of the inaugural cities of the new Israel Baseball League. The name of its team — The Modi'in Miracles of course!

Each day after school Orly and Anat practice running to build up their stamina. One day, Ima gets a call from Avi with a special request. After seeing the old photo, he's had an idea.

Finally, Hanukkah eve arrives. Avi drops the runners off at their different stations. Spectators have already gathered. Orly's eyes search for her parents, but they are nowhere to be found. Fifteen minutes later, Avi is back. As he carefully prepares the torch, Orly notices a white van pulling up. Ima gets out and whispers something to Avi. Abba opens the back door of the van and slowly Savta Raba gets out. With the help of her cane, she makes her way to Orly. "*Kadima!*" she calls out. "Go forward!"

"*Kadima*," urges Avi. "You're carrying a torch and a tradition… and there will be *sufganiot* – Hanukkah jelly doughnuts – for everyone, including Savta Raba, at the end of the relay."

Sufganiot

Ingredients

2 packages of dry yeast
4 Tbsp. sugar
$^3/_4$ c. water
1 egg and 1 egg yolk
$1^1/_2$ Tbsp. soft margarine
$2^1/_2$ c. sifted flour
1 tsp. vanilla extract
Dash of salt
Vegetable oil for frying
Your favorite berry jelly
Confectioner's sugar

Preparation

1. Dissolve yeast and sugar in water. Let the mixture stand for 10–12 minutes.

2. Place the flour in a bowl and make a hole in the middle. Add the yeast mixture, eggs, salt, vanilla, and margarine. Knead well.

3. Place the dough in a greased bowl. Cover it, refrigerate, and let it rise over night.

4. Sprinkle a board with flour. Roll the dough out flat. Use a cookie cutter or glass to cut out circles in the dough. Cover and let them rise for 10–15 minutes.

5. Roll each circle into a ball. Make a hole in the ball and put in a teaspoon of jam. Pinch the hole closed and flatten the ball.

6. In a deep pan, heat 2–3 inches of oil until it crackles. Drop balls into the pan a few at a time. Do not crowd. Turn them until they're golden brown on all sides. Cool on a paper towel. Sprinkle with confectioner's sugar.

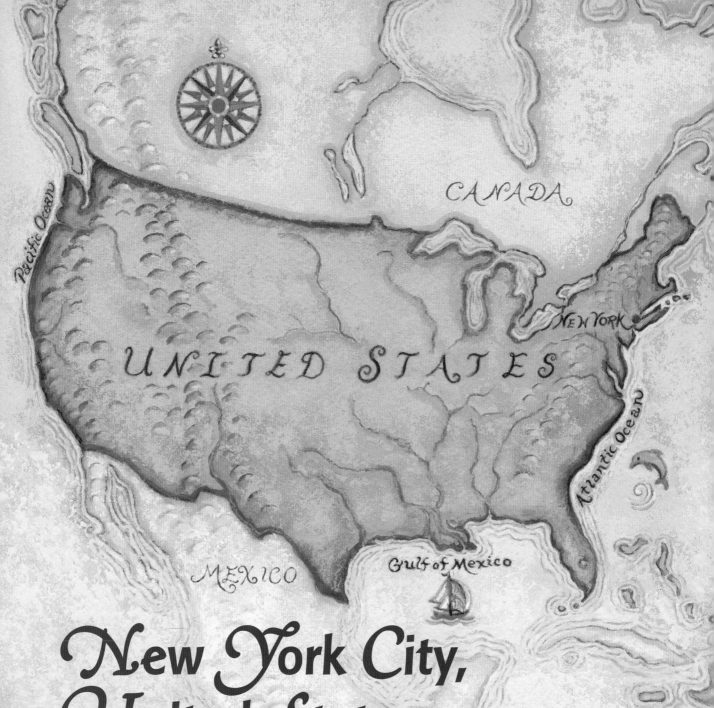

New York City, United States

Something Different Every Day

"Kids," calls Mom. "It's time to make the Hanukkah wheel."

Alicia comes into the kitchen, holding Joey. Next Adam pops in, with Shira right behind.

"We have a week until Hanukkah," Mom reminds them. "I've drawn the wheel. Let's decide what we'll do this year. We always bake cookies on the first night. Who has an idea for the second night?"

"Invite Grandma and Grandpa," Adam offers. "They play dreidel the best — and they use real money."

"Let's make night three a family music night," suggests Alicia. "Shira can play the recorder, Uncle Alan, the guitar, Cousin Karen, the clarinet, and Joey can bang on his bongo drums. Everyone else can sing along."

Turning the wheel Mom continues, "Each of you can invite a friend to sleep over on night four. Any suggestions for night five?"

"A movie," insists Adam.

"You're on," laughs Mom. "That brings us to night six."

"The JCC is having a Hanukkah party that night," Alicia reminds them. Mom nods. "And night seven is for tzedakah. Any ideas?"

"Let's go to Children's Hospital," Shira suggests. "We can play games, read stories, and bring balloons and gifts."

Adam stands up. "That brings us to night eight — BIG GIFT NIGHT."

"I knew you wouldn't forget that one," Mom laughs.

Hanukkah finally arrives. Every day the children turn the wheel to see what's scheduled. However, when it's time to light the candles, they always have to wait for Shira.

"Why can't you be on time?" Mom asks.

Shira blushes. "There's something I have to do first."

After Israel, the United States has the largest Jewish community in the world. Its history can be traced back to 1654, when a small group of Jews from Recife, Brazil, landed in New Amsterdam — now New York City. However, there is speculation that Jews fleeing the Spanish Inquisition were among the sailors who traveled with Columbus. For Jews around the world, the United States has always been the land of religious freedom and economic opportunity. Immigrants have come from Europe, South America, Asia, and the Middle East. The American Jewish poet Emma Lazarus, a Sephardic Jew whose ancestors came from Spain, wrote "The New Colossus," the famous poem welcoming newcomers, which is engraved on the Statue of Liberty.

At last BIG GIFT NIGHT arrives. Adam is excited. "I've been waiting for this night for over a week!"

Just as they are about to light the candles, the doorbell rings.

Shira opens the door and finds herself face-to-face with Mrs. Greenberg, their upstairs neighbor. She's holding a plate of Hanukkah cookies. "Such a wonderful daughter you have," she says, turning to Mom, who looks puzzled. "Shira has come to my apartment every night to light Hanukkah candles with me, so I wouldn't be alone. Tonight I decided to come to her…that is, if you don't mind."

"Of course not," stammers Mom. "Please join us." Walking over to Shira, she gives her a hug and whispers, "You just gave me the biggest gift of all."

Hanukkah Cookies

Ingredients

1 egg
1 c. sugar
½ c. butter or margarine
1 tsp. vanilla extract
¼ c. milk
2 tsp. baking powder
½ tsp. salt
2 c. flour

Preparation

1. Cream the butter, sugar, vanilla and egg until smooth.

2. Add the milk and mix again.

3. Add baking powder and salt and mix again.

4. Slowly add the flour and mix until fully blended.

5. Cover the dough in the bowl and refrigerate for an hour.

6. Sprinkle a cutting board with flour. Roll out the dough and cut out dreidel and other Hanukkah-shaped cookies with a cookie cutter or knife.

7. Place cookies on a greased cookie sheet and bake in a preheated 375°F oven for 8–10 minutes, or until they are golden.

8. Decorate your cookies with frosting and sprinkles.

Istanbul, Turkey ⛵

"Ocho Candelikas"

Molly is daydreaming about burmelos, the fried fritters that she's going to help Madre make for Hanukkah, when her brother Joseph suddenly marches into her room, interrupting her thoughts.

"Hurry up," he calls. "We have to get to the synagogue to rehearse. I hope you remember the words."

Molly sighs. Every day it's the same. Since Joseph was appointed head of the youth choir, he had become so self-important.

As they enter the synagogue, Menni, their choirmaster, is already lining up the children on the bimah. "Joseph," he commands, "stand next to me, so you can give the cues. Molly, I want you in the middle of the first row." Turning to face the 35 boys and girls, he counts to three, then points his finger. The children begin singing their favorite Ladino Hanukkah song:

"Hanukah linda sta aki, ocho
candelas para mi,
Hanukah linda sta aki, ocho
candelas para mi. O…"

Beautiful Hanukkah is here,
eight candles for me.

The choir continues, counting:

"Una candelika, dos candelikas,
tres candelikas,
kuatro candelikas,
sintyu candelikas,
sej candelikas,
siete candelikas,
ocho candelas para mi."

One candle, two candles,
three candles, four candles,
five candles, six candles,
seven candles, eight candles for me.

According to Jewish tradition, Noah's Ark landed on Mount Ararat, a mountain range in modern Turkey. We do know that Jews have lived in the area since the time of the Bible. The greatest immigration of Jews to Turkey was in the 15th century, when the Sultan issued a formal invitation to those Jews expelled from Spain and Portugal, to make the Ottoman Empire their home. Since then, the Jews in Turkey have enjoyed religious tolerance and prosperity, and suffered bad times as well. Today, 26,000 Jews live in Turkey, mostly in Istanbul. It was one of the first Muslim countries to recognize Israel, and the two countries work together in many ways. Turkey is a favorite vacation spot for Israelis.

Joseph holds out his hand, matching his fingers to each candle they count. Using him as their cue, the children raise their fingers in unison.

"Excellent." Menni claps when they finish. Winking at Molly, he adds, "You must be proud of your big brother."

The night of the festival arrives. As usual, Joseph urges Molly to hurry. Just as he yells out, "M-O-L-L-Y!" she comes out of the pantry.

"I'm ready," she smiles, hiding her hands in her skirt pockets.

The children file into the sanctuary, taking their places in front of the Ark. The girls are wearing white blouses, and the boys are wearing crisp, white shirts with bowties. Parents and grandparents enter the synagogue and sit in the men's and women's sections.

"One, two, three," whispers Menni to the children. They begin singing. Looking at Joseph, they raise their hands and start to count.

Just then, Molly steps forward. As the children sing: "Una candelika…," she reaches into her pocket, takes out a candle, and holds it up high. Then she holds two, then three…until she's holding all eight up in the air. The audience starts to applaud. "Bravo!" they call out.

Molly winks at Menni. "Thank you for letting me do that," she whispers. Turning to Joseph, she asks with a big grin, "Aren't you proud of your little sister?"

Molly's Burmelos

Ingredients

1 egg
1 c. milk
1 tsp. ground cinnamon
1 tsp. baking powder
11/2 c. flour
Oil
Your favorite syrup (maple, chocolate, etc.)

Preparation

1. Crack an egg into a bowl. Mix the egg well with a fork. Add the milk and mix again.

2. Add cinnamon and baking powder and mix again.

3. Slowly pour in the flour and mix until thick.

4. Heat oil in a deep frying pan. Drop the batter by tablespoons into the oil, keeping the fritters a few inches apart.

5. Turn them until they are golden brown on both sides.

6. Remove them from the oil and let drain on a paper towel.

7. Put them on a plate and top with syrup.

Samarkand, Uzbekistan
Dancing at Eight Family Feasts

"Abigai, Esther, I'm waiting for you in the kitchen."

"Coming, Bivi," the two girls call. Abigai and Esther live in Samarkand. Bivi is their grandma on their father's side.

Tonight is the first night of Hanukkah and the family will sit down to the first of eight festive family meals. Uncles Minash and Yacob will be there along with their families. But Aunts Mazal and Shoshana will celebrate in the homes of their husbands' families. In Uzbekistan, it is customary for sons to bring their families to their parents' homes to celebrate the first night of the holiday.

Bivi is getting impatient. She wants the girls to help her prepare *jarkoff*, the traditional Uzbekistan dish served on holidays. "I'm waiting!" she calls again.

"One minute," the girls giggle, tying bells around their wrists.

"What's that jingling?" Bivi asks them, when they come into the kitchen.

Holding their hands up in the air, the girls gracefully turn their wrists to the left, then the right.

Smiling, Bivi convinces them to remove the bells and help her peel potatoes. As they work, they clap their hands, snap their fingers, and tap their feet to the beat of a song.

"You must be up to something," insists Bivi. She hands them tomatoes. Abigai chops, while Esther stirs, moving her head back and forth. The two look at the clock, and as soon as they are finished, they run out the door.

Back home, Ona, their mother, is filling bags with candy for her nieces and nephews. The kitchen smells of freshly baked cake. Abigai and Esther rush in and head straight for their room.

"What are you girls doing?" calls Ona.

"You'll see," Esther answers.

As dusk begins to fall, Dadda, Bobo (their grandfather), and their uncles leave for synagogue. They will join the women and children afterward.

Local tradition claims that the Jewish community of Bukhara, the oldest in Uzbekistan, was established 2,000 years ago, after the destruction of the Temple in Jerusalem. Some say that the Jews who arrived there had fled Persia. Others say that they were Jewish merchants who were traveling on the Silk Road to China. Most were artisans and merchants, since land ownership was forbidden to Jews. Over the last centuries, they lived under a variety of rulers, not all of whom were friendly. Today, approximately 25,000 Jews remain in the newly-independent republic of Uzbekistan, residing in the cities of Bukhara, Samarkand, and Tashkent. These communities enjoy many Jewish activities and communal services.

When they finally gather, Bobo lights the hanukkiah for the family, and they sit down for dinner. Everyone compliments Bivi on the delicious food.

"Abigai and Esther helped me prepare *jarkoff*," she admits. The family turns to thank the girls, but they're not in their seats. Suddenly, music is in the air. Dressed in colorful costumes, the girls make a grand entrance, moving to the beat of the *besh karsak* folk dance.

"I knew you were up to something," grins Bivi, getting up to join her granddaughters. Within minutes, everybody is up, laughing and dancing. While they whirl and sway, Uncle Minash calls out, "My house, tomorrow night!" Smiling at his nieces he adds, "And I expect a different dance."

Bivi's Jarkoff

Ingredients

2 Tbsp. oil
½ chicken, cut and skinned
1 lb. potatoes, peeled and quartered
3 medium tomatoes, chopped
Dash of spices: salt, black
    pepper, and cumin
1 c. water

Preparation

1. Heat oil in a medium-sized pot and brown chicken.

2. Add potatoes and fry until golden.

3. Stir in tomatoes and spices.

4. Add water, bring to a boil, then lower flame to medium.

5. Cover the pot halfway and cook for 30 minutes.

6. Serve hot.

Turin, Italy

Connecting Tisha B'Av with Hanukkah

Jacopo is feeling proud. He's eight years old and for the first time his father, Alberto, is taking him to the synagogue on the night before Tisha B'Av.

"We are going to read a very sad story," explains Padre. "On the ninth day of the month of Av, the First and Second Temples in Jerusalem were destroyed, but we end the reading with a feeling of hope." Padre pauses, then asks, "Do you have our candle?"

Jacopo nods, digging deep into his right pocket to make sure the candle hasn't fallen out. Padre told him they are going to do something special with it. He can't wait.

They wind their way to the synagogue on Piazzetta Primo Levi. It's a huge building with four onion-shaped domes. Padre and Jacopo go into the side entrance, making their way down a narrow, semi-circular stairwell to a small chapel, decorated in blue and gold. Padre tells him it used to be the bakery where the community made its Passover matzah.

Padre asks Jacopo for the candle. He puts it into a small candleholder, stands it on the floor, and then lights it.

"Jacopo, come down on the floor next to me," says Padre, as he sits next to the candle.

By candlelight Padre reads *Eicha* (the Book of Lamentations) to Jacopo. "Now blow out the candle," Padre whispers when he's finished. Then Padre takes the burnt candle out of its holder and carefully wraps it in silver foil. He gives it to Jacopo to put back in his pocket.

The first Jews in Italy were ambassadors sent by Judah Maccabee in 161 BCE to forge an alliance against the Greeks. After the destruction of the Temple by Rome, Jews were brought to Italy as slaves. With the establishment of Christianity as the official religion, the Jews were often oppressed, though their fate depended on the particular Pope and ruler. About 20 percent of Italy's Jews were killed during the Holocaust. Today there are 40,000 Jews, mostly in the major cities of Rome, Florence, and Venice.

"What happens to the candle next?" asks a surprised Jacopo.

"What Jewish month is it?" Padre asks.

"Av," Jacopo answers.

Padre continues. "How many months until Kislev?"

"Four, but so what?" puzzles Jacopo.

Padre continues his questions. "What holiday do we celebrate in Kislev?"

Now Jacopo rolls his eyes. "Hanukkah! But what's the connection?"

Padre smiles. "Tonight we mourn the destruction of the Holy Temple, but on Hanukkah we celebrate its rededication. The candle we just used will connect the two events. Tonight it is a sad candle, but in four months' time, it will be a happy one."

Wide-eyed, Jacopo asks, "Will there be another miracle? Will the candle burn for eight nights just like the small jar of oil?"

"Not exactly," Padre, answers, "But this candle is our message of hope. It's saying, 'Remember the Temple was destroyed today on Tisha B'Av, but on Hannukah we regained our independence. Put me away and use me as the *shamash* — the helper candle for lighting the hanukkiah each night.'"

When they arrive home, Jacopo puts the wrapped candle near their hanukkiah and begins his countdown: "One hundred and thirty-three days to go!"

Hanukkah Precipizi

Ingredients

1 egg
1 Tbsp. sugar
1 Tbsp. flour
1 Tbsp. extra virgin olive oil
1 Tbsp. Cherry Heering brandy
Honey
Powdered sugar for topping
Olive oil for frying

Preparation

1. Mix all the ingredients until smooth.

2. Form into balls and fry in hot oil until golden brown. Drain the balls on a paper towel.

3. Pour enough honey into a saucepan to cover the balls (about 1 cup). Heat the honey, add balls to pot, and stir until the balls are coated with honey.

4. Pour the balls and honey onto an oiled cookie sheet. The balls should be touching, but not on top of each other. Oil a knife and cut into bars or squares. Move bars onto a second oiled cookie sheet to cool and harden. Dust with powdered sugar.

Sydney, Australia

Hanukkah in the Park

A hot breeze fans Michelle's face as she makes her way to the Great Synagogue. It's the end of the school year, and the rabbi has asked her to help plan the booths for the community's favorite summer event – Hanukkah in the Park.

Crossing through Hyde Park, Michelle remembers last year's carnival. The theme was *the Outback*. "I wonder what this year's theme will be," she muses.

As she nears the synagogue, she sees her friend Nicole waving.

"Michelle, hurry up. The rabbi just told us we're going to have snow this year for Hanukkah."

Michelle cannot believe her ears.

"That's right! This year's theme is going to be *Hanukkah in New York*."

"But the temperature can reach 100 degrees here," protests Michelle. "The snow will melt!"

"The rabbi will explain," Nicole assures her.

The committee was meeting in the rabbi's study. "Since Hanukkah in the Park has become such a popular citywide event," he explains, "the city council has given its approval for us to bring in snow."

"Won't it melt?" asks Michelle.

The first Europeans to settle in Australia in the late 18th century were convicts, and Jewish criminals were among them. Once gold was discovered on Australian shores in the 1850s, Australia fast became a land of opportunity, attracting many more immigrants, including Jews. Later, Eastern European Jews fled pogroms and made Australia their home, as did German refugees in the 1930s and after the Holocaust. Today, Australia's Jewish community numbers 100,000. Most live in Melbourne and Sydney.

"Not right away," the rabbi answers. "We'll make the snow the way they do it at ski resorts — by cooling the water just above its freezing point, and pumping it under high pressure through nozzles of a snow gun. It will last long enough to have snowball fights and a snow sculpture contest."

"What else is happening?" Michelle asks.

"The adult activities are lined up. We have a klezmer band that will play Hanukkah music and there will be craft stands and bookstalls," Nicole reports. "But we've got to help decide what to do for the kids!"

"No problem," smiles Kevin. "A rock climbing wall is a must. And let's rent a giant jumping castle."

"How about a boomerang toss and a place for face-painting?" suggests Sandra.

"And 'Bounce Eye,'" adds Nicole. "Everyone loves that marble game."

"We can't forget to order prizes," insists Marcus.

"You're very quiet," says the rabbi, turning to Michelle.

"I'm thinking about food," she replies. "Will we have electrical outlets?"

"Yes. What do you have in mind?"

A grin slowly crosses Michelle's face. "I'll show you tonight when we light the giant hanukkiah on Bondi Beach."

Michelle arrives at the candlelighting carrying a tall, insulated cup, with a straw poking through the cover. After the community finishes singing *Maoz Tzur* she turns to the rabbi. "Have a sip!" she says.

"Refreshing!" he exclaims. "What is it?"

"New Yorkers call it a Blizzard – but they drink it in the summer!"

Michelle's New York Blizzard

Ingredients

3 small scoops vanilla ice cream

1 c. ice cubes

¼ c. milk

2 tsp. sugar

1 tsp. vanilla extract

Preparation

Place all the ingredients in a blender and blend until mixture is the consistency of snow.

North Sea

Baltic Sea

POLAND

★ WARSAW

EUROPE

Mediterranean Sea

Warsaw, Poland
The Competition

Mateusz can't believe his ears. His tata (father) has just asked him to explain the story of Hanukkah. "Tata, this is the first time I know something that you don't," he giggles bashfully.

Tata smiles. "That's why Babcia (Grandma) enrolled you in the Lauder-Morasha School."

Babcia was born in Warsaw, but she and her family escaped to Russia when the Nazis came. After the war the family returned.

Mateusz remembers the first day Babcia took him to school.

"I can't believe I'm here," his grandmother told the principal. "A Jewish school in Warsaw, Poland. Who would have thought? My grandson will have the chance to learn what it means to be a Jew. His father missed that opportunity."

Mateusz finishes telling his father the story of the Maccabees, then adds, "We're having a competition at school. There will be a special prize for the best hanukkiah."

"But we don't have one to enter in the contest," Tata says.

"We have to make our own," Mateusz replies. "We can ask our parents to help and since you're a potter, I thought we could make ours out of clay. You can shape it, I can paint it, then we can glaze it, and…"

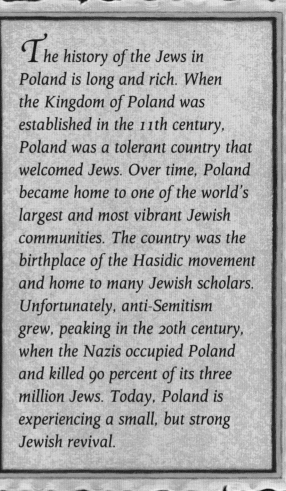

The history of the Jews in Poland is long and rich. When the Kingdom of Poland was established in the 11th century, Poland was a tolerant country that welcomed Jews. Over time, Poland became home to one of the world's largest and most vibrant Jewish communities. The country was the birthplace of the Hasidic movement and home to many Jewish scholars. Unfortunately, anti-Semitism grew, peaking in the 20th century, when the Nazis occupied Poland and killed 90 percent of its three million Jews. Today, Poland is experiencing a small, but strong Jewish revival.

"And even if we don't win, we win, because we did it together. It will be fun," his father agrees.

It takes Mateusz and Tata over a week to create the right design and shape. "Don't forget the *shamash*," reminds Mateusz, as Tata molds each branch. Mateusz paints the hanukkiah white and trims it with blue. Tata adds a touch of gold paint here and there. "Do you think we'll win?" Mateusz asks anxiously.

"We'll have to wait and see," answers Tata.

On the day of the competition, Mateusz can't sit still. His class gathers in the school auditorium where the hanukkiot are lined up on a table. Mateusz watches as the principal and teachers go up and down the row, writing numbers on their pads. Once they tally the scores they show them to the Chief Rabbi of Warsaw, who is sitting on the podium. "Third place goes to Hanna and her family," the rabbi announces as everyone applauds. "Second place goes to Zofia and her family," he continues. Mateusz turns to his father, tears in his eyes. "We're never going to win," he says, running out of the room.

The rabbi sees Mateusz leave the hall. "Next week I am going to present the winning hanukkiah to Poland's president," he says proudly. "But I can't announce the winner, because not everyone is in the room. Mr. Zimbrofsky, please get your son back in here. I think he should be present when the winner's name is called out."

Babcia's Potato Latkes

Ingredients

4 large potatoes, peeled
1 egg
Dash of salt and pepper
2 Tbsp. white flour
Oil for frying
Sour cream or apple sauce
   for topping

Preparation

1. Grate the potatoes, let stand for 10 minutes, and drain liquid.

2. Mix in salt, pepper, egg, and flour.

3. Preheat oil in frying pan until very hot. Drop tablespoons of batter
into pan, and fry until golden brown on both sides.

4. Drain on a paper towel and serve hot with applesauce or
sour cream.

Nabeul, Tunisia

Honoring Brave Judith

It's cold and wet on the streets of Paris, but Jacqueline, Geannette, Danielle, and Margot are enjoying the toasty warmth of their Grand-mère's home. The cousins have already lit the candles for the seventh night of Hanukkah. Grand-mère explains that this night is for girls only, the way it was in Nabeul, Tunisia, where she grew up.

"Hanukkah is the only holiday that starts in one Hebrew month, Kislev, and ends in another, Tevet," Grand-mère explains. "Tonight is *Rosh Chodesh*, the beginning of the new month. When I grew up, the Rosh Chodesh that fell during Hanukkah was a holiday within a holiday. It was called *Chag haBanot*, Festival of the Daughters."

Algiers

Tunis

Nabeul

Mediterranean Sea

TUNISIA

Tripoli

"And you slept over at your Grand-mère's house?" asks Jacqueline.

"We did more than that. While the candles burned, we relaxed. No one went into the kitchen. The next day we had a feast for women and girls *only*."

"No annoying boys?" asks a wide-eyed Geannette.

"We did serve them a snack after candlelighting – an artichoke, olive spread, or a hard-boiled egg. But the really delicious food was saved for the women's feast, where young and old gathered to honor Judith, the Hanukkah heroine."

"I don't remember a Maccabee named Judith," insists Margot.

"Aha! I knew one of you would say that. Legend has it that the Maccabees were inspired by Judith's bravery. Who knows her story?"

"I do," says Danielle. "Judith fed a Syrian Greek general salty cheese that made him thirsty, so she gave him wine to drink. He got drunk and then she …"

"Stop," insists Grand-mère. "I'll tell you the *whole* story tomorrow at the celebration. And I want each one of you to tell a story, too -- about a different Jewish heroine."

"Is that what you did?" asks Jacqueline.

*J*ews have lived in Tunisia since the destruction of the First Temple. The first Jews were divided into clans, working in agriculture, cattle-raising, and trade. Over the centuries, they lived under the influence of many conquerors: Muslim Arabs, Spaniards, Turks, and French colonizers. In the 19th century life was hard for Tunisian Jews. They were discriminated against and forced to pay a special tax. Their houses and synagogues had to be lower than those of their Arab neighbors. Life improved once the French colonized Tunisia in 1881. However, during World War II, Tunisia was the only Arab country to come under direct Nazi occupation, requiring the Jews to wear Star of David badges and sending them to forced labor camps. Once Tunisia became independent in 1956, the government closed the Jewish Community Council and the Jews began leaving for France or Israel. Today the Jewish community numbers around 1,500.

"Oui," answers Grand-mère. "We had heard enough stories about heroes. On the seventh day of Hanukkah we honored only our heroines: Sarah, Rivka, Rachel, Miriam, Judith, Hannah, and…"

"And that's it?" interrupts Geannette rudely. Danielle frowns at her. Geannette frowns back.

"That reminds me of another thing we did," adds Grand-mère. "We settled all fights and apologized to one another."

"Sorry," says a half-hearted Danielle.

"Anything else?" continues Geannette.

"At the end of the meal we ate special *Debla* cookies. We'll bake some tomorrow."

"No entertainment?" asks Margot.

"Of course," smiles Grand-mère. "We danced and listened to all the popular songs."

"Sung by women?"

"Naturally."

Grand-mère pauses, gets up from her seat, and goes over to a table with drawers. "One last thing. One year my Grand-mère gave me four pieces of her favorite jewelry. Guess who's going to get them tonight?"

Debla Cookies

Ingredients

2 eggs
1¼ c. flour
Pinch of salt
Oil for frying

Topping:
1 c. water
½ c. sugar
1 Tbsp. lemon juice

Preparation

1. Crack open two eggs in a large mixing bowl.

2. Beat eggs and add flour and salt. Stir to combine, then knead into a dough.

3. Roll the dough thin and cut into strips 1 inch wide.

4. Using a fork, twist each strip into a circle.

5. Heat oil in a deep frying pan and fry each circle separately. It will puff up and open like a rose. Once it opens and is golden brown, remove it from the pan and drain on a paper towel.

6. Mix the topping ingredients together and cook until thickened.

7. Drizzle over the roses.

Hanukkah Potpourri

For the past 2,000 years, Jews have lived in many nations, often adapting local customs into their holiday celebrations. Here are a few:

Aleppo, Syria

The Jews of Aleppo were descendants of Sephardic Jews expelled from Spain in 1492. When they finally found a safe haven in Syria, they vowed to light an additional *shamash* on Hanukkah as a sign of thanks. And that's not all! Each morning of Hanukkah they lit twelve oil lamps, one for each of the twelve tribes. There is no longer a Jewish community in Syria, but the tradition continues among their descendants.

Bergen-Belsen Concentration Camp, Germany

In 1943, Jewish inmates of the Bergen-Belsen concentration camp were determined to celebrate Hannukah. The men saved up bits of fat from their small food portions. The women pulled out threads from their tattered clothing and twisted them into makeshift wicks. They transformed half of a raw potato into a candleholder. Dreidels were carved out of their wooden shoes, and given to the dozen children in the camp. Risking their lives, the prisoners made their way to Barrack 10 on the first night of Hanukkah, where a Hasidic rabbi conducted a candlelighting ceremony, giving these poor, suffering Jews a sense of spiritual strength similar to that found in the story of the Maccabees.

France

The Jews of Avignon in southern France, known for their wine-making and cooking talents, open new casks of wine on the evening following Shabbat Hanukkah. They make their way from home to home, sampling the new wine and toasting the holiday. French Jews savor sugar-dusted *beignets*, a deep-fried pastry also popular in New Orleans.

Israel

In 1958, the Bank of Israel began to mint special commemorative coins to be used as Hannukah gelt. The first coin featured the same hannukiah that appeared on the last Maccabean coin issued 1,998 years earlier. Each year's new coin honors a different Jewish community around the world.

Kurdistan

While Jews no longer live in Kurdistan, many Kurdish Jews still observe two unusual Hanukkah customs. The first is reminiscent of the giving of Hanukkah gelt. A week before the holiday, children lock the doors to their rooms. Parents are allowed entry only after offering coins. The second custom was developed by Jews too poor to afford a hanukkiah. They used eggshells as cups for wicks and oil, lighting the required number of cracked shells every night.

Mexico

In Mexico, the festival of lights is called "*Januca*." Children play *toma todo* — a game of dreidel— but the highlight of their celebration is breaking a piñata shaped like a dreidel and collecting sweets and toys.

Morocco

In Morocco, each family gathers all the remaining wicks and oil at the end of the holiday and makes a bonfire.

Spain

In 1998, 500 years after the Jews were expelled from Spain, the country celebrated its first Hanukkah in the city of Gerona. Over 1,000 people attended, including Israel's Chief Sephardic Rabbi. Gerona is a medieval city that was once home to an important school of kabbalah. In fact, Rabbi Nissim of Gerona was the first to connect the story of Judith to Hannukah. Today, Gerona's Jewish ghetto, which is called a "call", is one of the best preserved medieval ghettos in Europe.

Tunisia

There are 1,500 Jews still living in Tunisia. Each family hangs its hanukkiah on the doorpost opposite the mezuzah. The oil and wicks are homemade. Women do not do any work during the time that the lights burn. The hanukkiah remains on the door-post until Purim.

United States

"The Great Latke-Hamantash Debate," originated at the University of Chicago, has become a popular tradition both on campuses and in communities around the country. In good fun and often with elaborate visual aids, people argue, discuss, and debate the merits of latkes vs. hamantaschen on the basis of nutritional, psychological, sociological, and other criteria.

Glossary

All words are Hebrew unless otherwise noted.

Abba – father

Babcia – grandmother (Polish)

Bimah – central podium in the synagogue

Bivi – grandmother (Uzbek)

Bobo – grandfather (Uzbek)

Burmelos – fried fritters eaten by Sephardic Jews

Chag Ha-Banot – Holiday of the Daughters

Chag Ha-Or – Holiday of Light

Dadda - father (Uzbek)

Dreidel – spinning top (Yiddish); called sevivon in Hebrew

Grand-mère – grandmother (French)

Hamantaschen – three-cornered pastry eaten on Purim

Hanukkah – eight-day holiday recalling the victory of the Jews against the Syrians

Hanukkat Ha-bayit – literally "rededication of the house," a housewarming celebration that includes affixing a mezuzah to a home

Hanukkiah – nine-branched candelabra used on Hanukkah (plural is hanukkiot)

Hasidic – ultra religious sect of Jews

Havdalah – ceremony ending Shabbat

Ima – mother

Jarkoff – holiday stew eaten in Uzbekistan

Kabbalah – Jewish mysticism

Kislev – Hebrew month in which Hanukkah is celebrated

Ladino – Judeo-Spanish language

Latkes – pancakes (Yiddish) eaten on Hanukkah by Ashkenazi Jews

Maccabees – Jewish resistance fighters whose victory is celebrated on Hanukkah

Matzah – unleavened bread eaten on Passover

Menorah – candelabra

Mezuzah – parchment with Biblical verses, affixed to doorpost of house

Ona – mother (Uzbek)

Oui – yes (French)

Padre – father (Italian)

Passover – holiday celebrating the Exodus of the Israelite slaves from Egypt

Pinata – brightly colored paper container filled with candy and toys used on celebrations

Purim – holiday celebrating the victory of the Persian Jews over evil Haman

Rabbi – Jewish religious leader

Rosh Chodesh – monthly celebration of the new moon

Savta raba – great-grandmother

Shabbat – Sabbath

Shamash – helper candle used to light all others in hanukkiah

Sufganiot – jelly donuts eaten on Hanukkah in Israel

Talmud – compilation of Jewish law and lore

Tata – father (Polish/Yiddish)

Tisha B'Av – the 9th of Av, a memorial day to the destruction of the Holy Temples in Jerusalem

Torah – The Five Books of Moses

Tzedakah – charitable contribution

About the Author

Tami Lehman-Wilzig is the author of several children's books including *Passover Around the World, Tasty Bible Stories,* and *Keeping the Promise: A Torah's Journey,* an International Reading Association's Teacher's Choice Award winner. She lives in Petach Tikvah, Israel.

About the Illustrator

Vicki Wehrman attended Washington University School of Fine Arts in St. Louis, Missouri, where she studied painting, drawing and printmaking. She lives in the Rochester, New York, area with her husband, illustrator Richard Wehrman.